PRIVATE EYE

COVER~UP!

Published by Private Eye Productions Limited
6 Carlisle Street, London W1
in association with André Deutsch Limited
105 Great Russell Street, London WC1

©Pressdram Limited

ISBN 0 233 98475 5
Printed in Great Britain by Ebenezer Baylis & Son Limited, Worcester

The birth of Prince Henry (Harry).

PRIVATE EYE

No. 594
Friday
21 Sept. '84

40p

ROYAL BABY

EXCLUSIVE PICTURE

The Labour leader makes a
personal revelation.

PRIVATE EYE

No. 586
Friday
1 June '84

40p

NEIL GIMMOCK: VASECTOMY SHOCK

BAD
TASTE
SPECIAL

Mark Thatcher goes to work in America.

PRIVATE EYE

No. 582
Friday
6 April '84

40p

The NUM seek assistance from Libya
in their dispute.

PRIVATE EYE

597
ay
ov. '84

40p

Gaddafi's no more mad than I am

The House of Lords is televised.

No. 602
Friday
5 Jan. '85

40p

PRIVATE EYE

⋆ LORDS ⋆ TV ⋆ SPECTACULAR ⋆

The miners' strike draws to a close.

PRIVATE EYE

No. 604
Friday
Feb. '85

40p

PIT STRIKE LATEST!

Civil servant Clive Ponting is acquitted of charges of breaking the Official Secrets Act.

PRIVATE EYE

No. 605
Friday
22 Feb. '85

40p

The miners' strike ends.

PRIVATE EYE

506
ay
rch '85

40p

MINERS CAVE IN!

Cecil Parkinson successfully injuncts Private Eye. He moves from the inside page to the front cover as the Eye immediately reprints.

PRIVATE EYE

606 A
ay
arch '85

40p

SPECIAL REPEAT ISSUE !

The Chancellor fails to convince everyone about the economy.

No. 607
Friday
March '85

40p

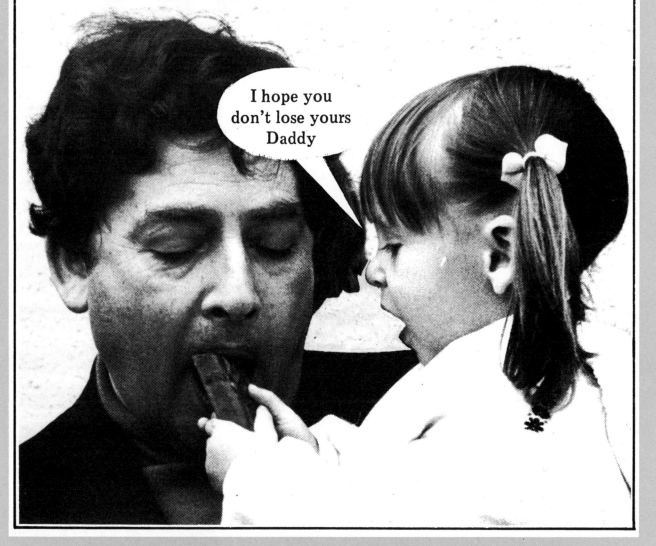

Mrs Thatcher is interviewed by David Frost.

PRIVATE EYE

613
ay
une '85

40p

MAGGIE IN TV SHOCK

Allegations surface about
Princess Michael of Kent.

PRIVATE EYE

No. 615
Friday July '85
40p

GERMAN'S WIMBLEDON TRIUMPH

President Reagan undergoes an operation
on his colon.

PRIVATE EYE

616
May July '85
40p

REAGAN AMAZING RECOVERY

Jeffrey Archer is appointed deputy chairman of the Conservative Party.

PRIVATE EYE

622
May
Oct. '85
40p

ARCHER SINGS THE BLUES

Prince Charles expresses concern about the plight of the unemployed.

No. 623
Friday
Nov. '85

PRIVATE EYE

40p

The US-Soviet summit opens
in Geneva.

PRIVATE EYE

624
ay
Nov. '85

40p

SUMMIT SOUVENIR ISSUE

Mrs Thatcher and Dr Garret Fitzgerald sign Anglo-Irish Agreement to the fury of Ulster protestants.

PRIVATE EYE

5

v. '85

40p

The Conservative Party attempts to
project a more compassionate image.

PRIVATE EYE

No. 637
Friday
16 May '86

40p

30 million people worldwide join in a charity event with the slogan 'I ran the world'. Denis Thatcher is not one of them.

PRIVATE EYE

638
ay
May '86

40p

SPORTS AID SPECIAL

High hopes are disappointed as
England are knocked out of the
World Cup in Mexico.

639
day
June '86

PRIVATE EYE

45p

Foreign Secretary Geoffrey Howe is sent
on a visit to South Africa.

PRIVATE EYE

No. 640
Friday
27 June '86

45p

BOTHA
HOWE
GETS TOUGH

ON OTHER PAGES: NOTHING

Debate rages in the Church of England over the ordination of women.

PRIVATE EYE

No. 641
Friday
July '86

45p

Reports of conflict between Mrs Thatcher and the Queen (right) over sanctions against South Africa emerge during the Commonwealth Games.

PRIVATE EYE

No. 642
Friday
July '86

45p

ROYAL COUPLE
SOUVENIR PICTURE

Commonwealth summit opens.

PRIVATE EYE

o. 643
riday
Aug. '86

45p

TALKS OPEN

Jeffrey Archer resigns as deputy chairman of the Conservative Party following allegations involving a prostitute.

649
ay
Oct. '86

PRIVATE EYE

45p

Speculation about a possible early
election increases.

PRIVATE EYE

No. 650
Friday
Nov. '86

ELECTION FEVER MOUNTS

Robert Maxwell sues Private Eye.
The Eye reacts with suitable penitence.

PRIVATE EYE

o. 651
riday
Nov. '86

45p

. . . and if they put me on the cover, I'll sue them again

HEALTH WARNING
THIS IS A DISEASED ORGAN AND MAY GIVE YOU AIDS
ISSUED BY ROBERT MAXWELL ON BEHALF OF HIMSELF

Royal frolics.

PRIVATE EYE

653
day
Dec. '86

45p

 Season's Greetings

James Anderton, Chief Constable of
Greater Manchester, claims that he may
be a prophet of God.

PRIVATE EYE

No. 655
Friday
23 Jan. '87

45p

GOD TALKS TO KNACKER

Mark Thatcher marries Texan heiress Diane Burgdorf.

PRIVATE EYE

657
ay
eb. '87

45p

Mrs Thatcher visits Moscow.

PRIVATE EYE

45p

YES, IT'S MOSCOW MAGGIE!

Neil Kinnock spells out a new
policy direction.

PRIVATE EYE

658
May
March '87
45p

LABOUR —
THE WAY FORWARD

Two of the Queen Mother's nieces are
revealed to have been in mental hospitals for
years although listed as dead.

PRIVATE EYE

o. 661
day
April '87.

45p

The security services come under criticism
after repeated scandals.

PRIVATE EYE

o. 662
riday
May '87.

45p

MI6 CLEAN UP

The two Davids decide that their joint appearances are not helping their electoral choices.

PRIVATE EYE

664
day
May '87

45p

The Conservative Party wins its third consecutive General Election.

PRIVATE EYE

565
y
ne '87

45p

SHOCK RESULT

It's a victory for common sense

In Jeffrey Archer's libel action against
the Star newspaper, prostitute
Monica Coghlan claims that Archer
has memorable acne.

PRIVATE EYE

668
May
July '87

45p

The Law Lords vote to ban Peter Wright's "Spycatcher".

No. 669
Friday
Aug. '87

PRIVATE EYE CATCHER

50p

**LATEST
LATEST
LATEST
LATEST
LATEST**

Owen forms 'breakaway' SDP.

PRIVATE EYE

. 671
day
ept. '87

50p

FOURTH PARTY SETS SAIL

Mrs Thatcher announces an inner-city initiative as a government priority.

PRIVATE EYE

672
day
Sept '87

50p

MAGGIE SEES INNER CITIES

Kinnock makes a controversial speech
at the Labour Party Conference.

PRIVATE EYE

673
May
ct. '87

50p

Cecil Parkinson returns to the Cabinet as Energy Secretary.

PRIVATE EYE

o. 674
iday
Oct. '87
50p

The Prince and Princess of Wales visit Germany amid speculation about their marriage.

PRIVATE EYE

o. 676
riday
Nov. '87

50p

ROYAL TOUR SOUVENIR

Delays in heart operations for children highlight cuts in the NHS.

. 679
day
Dec. '87

PRIVATE EYE

50p

SICK JOKE SPECIAL !

The Eye salutes Mrs Thatcher.

PRIVATE EYE

680
day
an. '88

50p

500 GLORIOUS YEARS

SOUVENIR ISSUE

Kurt Waldheim denies allegations of his Nazi war activities.

683
May
Feb. '88

PRIVATE EYE

50p

WALDHEIM SHOCK

The SDP/Liberal merger runs into trouble
as David Owen looks on.

PRIVATE EYE

681
day
Jan. '88

50p

MERGER CRISIS

The merger coincides with Red Nose Day.

PRIVATE EYE

682
lay
eb. '88

50p

COMIC RELIEF

Parkinson announces plan to sell off British Electricity to the private sector.

PRIVATE ISE

. 684
iday
March '88.

50p

CECIL'S TRIUMPH

Maxwell attempts to suppress Tom Bower's
biography "Maxwell, The Outsider"
through the publishers, the booksellers
and the publicists.

PRIVATE EYE

685
ay
March '88.

50p

MAXWELL BOOK ROW

Anyone who says I'm threatening them will get a writ

WARNING:
IT IS AN OFFENCE TO
LOOK AT THIS COVER

The Prime Minister declares war on litter.

. 686
day
April '88.

PRIVATE EYE

50p

APRIL FOOL

Questions over Zola Budd's British
nationality continue.

PRIVATE EYE

688
ay
April '88.

50p

ZOLA SPEAKS OUT

Major Ron Ferguson is rehabilitated after his disgrace over his activities in the Wigmore Club.

PRIVATE EYE

No. 691
Friday
June '88

50p

ROYAL PARDON

 SOUVENIR ISSUE

The US shoot down a civilian Iranian airbus over the Gulf.

PRIVATE EYE

o. 693
iday
uly '88

50p

TRAGIC ERROR – "IRAN TO BLAME"

The birth of Princess Beatrice.

PRIVATE EYE

696
May
Aug. '88
50p

ROYAL ISSUE
(Geddit?)

The Gibraltar Inquest questions the
role of the SAS.

. 698
day
Sept. '88

50p

Edwina Currie tells pensioners to wear
more clothes to combat cold.

699
ay
ept. '88

PRIVATE EYE

50p

EDWINA'S O.A.P. WINTER SHOCKER

Sarah Keays injuncts Norman Tebbit's book and the offending section is removed.

PRIVATE EYE

700
Friday
Oct. '88

50p

KEAYS GAGS TEBBIT

Koo Stark wins vast damages from the Star.
They alleged she continued to see Prince
Andrew after her marriage.

No. 702
Friday
11 Nov. '88

PRIVATE EYE

50p

Edwina Currie resigns after the furore over her remarks about salmonella.

PRIVATE EGG

05

y

ec. '88

50p

EDWINA QUITS

Mrs Thatcher appears rapidly at the scene of a number of catastrophes.

PRIVATE EYE

No. 707
Friday
Jan. '89

50p

The Prime Minister steps into the escalating crisis over food safety.

PRIVATE EYE

709
day
Feb. '89

50p

FOOD
THATCHER ACTS

If it wasn't contaminated, it is now

WARNING
Cook thoroughly before reading

Ayatollah Khomeini issues a death sentence on Salman Rushdie, author of "The Satanic Verses".